D0771367

T2-BPM-099

Sam Houston

A Leader for Texas

by Judy
Alter

Children's Press®
A Division of Grolier Publishing
New York London Hong Kong Sydney
Danbury, Connecticut

JB
HOUSTON

Photo Credits

Photographs ©: Brown Brothers: 34; Corbis-Bettmann: 7 inset, 28, 38, 40; Dave G. Houser: back cover, 6 (Rankin Harvey); Gilcrease Museum: 19; Greater Houston Convention and Visitor's Bureau: 43; Monkmeyer Press: 45 (Merrim); North Wind Picture Archives: 13, 24, 26; Photo Researchers: 10 (R.T. Nowitz Photos); Robert Fried: 27; Sam Houston Memorial Museum, Hustsville, TX: 8, 9 top, 14, 18, 25, 35, 37, 42; Sam Houston Regional Library and Research Center, Liberty, Texas: 2 (Jean Houston Baldwin Collection), 21 (Sam Houston Collection), 31; Smiley's Studio, Fort Worth, Texas: 48; Stock Montage, Inc.: cover; Texas Department of Transportation: 3, 23; Texas State Library, Archives & Information Services Division: 30 (Eric Beggs), 17, 36; Tony Stone Images: 7 top (Ron Sanford), 9 bottom, 44 (Bob Thompson).

Reading Consultant

Linda Cornwell, Learning Resource Consultant
Indiana Department of Education

Visit Children's Press on the Internet at:
http://publishing.grolier.com

Library of Congress Cataloging-in-Publication Data

Alter, Judy, 1938-
  Sam Houston : a leader for Texas / by Judy Alter.
    p. cm. — (Community builders)
  Includes bibliographical references and index.
  Summary: A biography of Sam Houston who served as a Congressman and Governor of Tennessee before his association with Texas began.
    ISBN: 0-516-20834-9 (lib. bdg.)   0-516-26331-5 (pbk.)
    1. Houston, Sam, 1793-1863—Juvenile literature. 2. Governors—Texas—Biography—Juvenile literature. 3. Legislators—United States—Biography—Juvenile literature. 4. United States. Congress. Senate—Biography—Juvenile literature. 5. Texas—History—To 1846—Juvenile literature. [1. Houston, Sam, 1793-1863. 2. Governors. 3. Legislators.] I. Title. II. Series.
F390.H84A66 1998
976.4'04'092—dc21
[B]
                                                                                        97-25199
                                                                                              CIP
                                                                                               AC

©1998 Children's Press®, a Division of Grolier Publishing Co., Inc.
All rights reserved. Published simultaneously in Canada.
Printed in the United States of America.
1 2 3 4 5 6 7 8 9 10 R 07 06 05 04 03 02 01 00 99 98

Contents

Chapter ONE

Texas

Texas, known for its huge size, covers almost 267,000 square miles (430,000 square kilometers).

Look at a map of the United States and find Texas. Its unusual shape may already be familiar to you. Texas is the second largest state (only Alaska is larger). Texas has eight million citizens. It also has two of the country's biggest and most important cities—Houston and Dallas. When you think of Texas, you might think of cowboys and cattle drives. Or perhaps you think about oil wells and barbed wire. But you may not know that without Sam Houston, Texas might be a Mexican state rather than a part of the United States.

Ranchers on horseback
rounding up cattle (above) and
oil wells (right) are some of the
things that come to mind when
people hear the word "Texas."

Sam Houston was a famous soldier and an honorary member of the Cherokee Indian nation. He was the commander in chief of the Texas army. He served as president of the Republic of Texas, and was a United States Senator. Sam Houston was also the only man ever to serve as the governor of two different states (Tennessee and Texas).

Sam Houston is regarded as a hero in U.S. history.

As a general in the Texas army, Sam Houston inspired Texans to fight for their independence from Mexico. He led the army that defeated the Mexicans in 1836. As president of the Republic of Texas, he saw that Texas became part of the United States. Because of all Sam Houston did for Texas, the city of Houston is named after him.

This street named for Sam Houston is located in Huntsville, Texas.

Most cities in Texas have a Houston Street. There is also the Sam Houston State University, the Sam Houston Memorial Museum and the Sam Houston Historical Park. All of these places are located in Huntsville, Texas, the town where Sam Houston lived.

Sam Houston Historical Park in Houston, Texas

A sunset view of the Shenendoah River Valley
of Virginia, where Sam was born

Chapter TWO

A Farm Boy and the Cherokee Indians

Sam Houston was born on March 2, 1793, in the Shenendoah River Valley in Virginia. He was the fifth of nine children born to Samuel Houston and his wife Elizabeth. Samuel Houston owned a plantation (a large farm), but he spent most of his time with the militia. The militia was a group of men who trained to fight in times of emergency. Sam's father spent so much time with the militia, he didn't pay attention to his plantation. As a result, the Houston family was poor.

By the time young Sam was fourteen years old, his father had died. Elizabeth Houston moved the family to Tennessee. Sam had little interest in either farming or school, but he liked to read books. When he was put to work in the family general store, he ran away to live with the Cherokee Indians.

Sam lived with the peaceful Cherokee led by Chief Oo-loo-te-ka. The chief was also known as

The Cherokee Indians

The Cherokee lived in the southern part of the United States. They lived in log cabins and farmed the land. In 1838, the United States government forced most of the tribe to walk from their homeland in the South to the plains of the Indian Territory (present-day Oklahoma). So many Cherokee died on the long trail that it is known as the Trail of Tears.

Not long after Sam Houston joined the Cherokee, he received an Indian name that means "The Raven."

John Jolly. When Sam joined the Cherokee, he received the Indian name Colonneh, which means "The Raven." (He was known as The Raven for the rest of his life.) Sam lived with the Cherokee for about two and a half years.

The small school Sam Houston started in Maryville, Tennessee, has been preserved for visitors.

In 1812, Sam Houston returned to his family. He opened a private school and earned enough money to pay off a small debt. When the War of 1812 began, he enlisted in the army as a private. His brothers thought it was disgraceful that Sam was not an officer. But Sam told them, "You don't know me now, but you shall hear of me."

After the war ended in 1815, Sam Houston was appointed the U.S. government's agent to deal with Indians in Tennessee. He knew the Indians and they trusted him. In 1817, a treaty granted more than 1,000,000 acres (405,000 hectares) of Cherokee land to the U.S. government. The treaty also required that the Cherokee move from Tennessee to the area that would later become Oklahoma and Arkansas.

The War of 1812

The United States declared war on Great Britain because British ships were stopping American ships at sea and taking their cargo. The British also encouraged Indian attacks on American settlers. In 1814, the British marched on Washington, D.C., and burned the White House. Early in 1815, the war ended.

Sam Houston went to the nation's capital, Washington, D.C., to protest the treaty. He tried to explain that the Indians were being treated unfairly. But Houston went to Washington dressed in Indian clothing—leather leggings, a beaded shirt, a blanket, and an Indian-style hat. No one would take his protest seriously because of the clothes he was wearing. Sam Houston was angered by this. As a result, he resigned from the army. But the trip to Washington set a pattern for one of his lifelong interests. Sam Houston always worked hard to see that the Indians were treated fairly. He tried to make sure that they were allowed to keep the land they lived on.

In this illustration from *The Life of Sam Houston*, published in 1860, Chief Oo-loo-te-ka (left) embraces Sam Houston (right) upon Houston's return from Washington, D.C., where he spoke on behalf of the Cherokee.

Chapter THREE

Soldier, Governor, Cherokee

Sam Houston was a Tennessee state representative.

After Sam Houston left the army, he went to Nashville, Tennessee, to learn about law. By 1818, he became a lawyer. In 1823, when he was only thirty years old, he was elected to the United States House of Representatives from Tennessee.

Just four years later, in 1827, Houston was elected governor of Tennessee. In 1829, he married for the first time. His wife was Eliza Allen. Within a few months, however, the couple separated.

Upset by the end of his marriage, Sam Houston resigned as governor of Tennessee. He rejoined John Jolly and the Cherokee. Everyone thought Houston's career as a politician was over.

John Jolly

Meanwhile, even though Sam Houston was not Cherokee, he was accepted as a member of the tribe. Once again, he traveled to Washington, D.C., to represent them. Houston's friend, President Andrew Jackson, promised to help the Indians keep their land.

Houston returned to present-day Arkansas and settled down with the Cherokee. He built a home and married a Cherokee named Tiana Rogers. Houston had a new wife, a good business as a trader, a respected role as an Indian spokesperson, and a newspaper column that he wrote for the *Arkansas Gazette.* But despite all this, Sam Houston wasn't happy. He drank too much whiskey. The Indians called him the "Big Drunk." No one thought he would ever again make anything of himself.

In 1832, Congressman William Stanbery published remarks that accused Houston of cheating the Indians out of food that the U.S. government had given to them. Sam was outraged. He demanded an explanation from Stanbery, but Stanbery did not reply. Houston was so angry, he said that he would attack Stanbery with a cane made from the hard wood of a hickory tree.

When the two men met on a street in Washington, D.C., Stanbery tried to fire a pistol at Houston. The pistol misfired. Houston then beat Stanbery with his hickory cane. The U.S. House of Representatives

Sam Houston's (left) fight with Congressman Stanbery was a turning point in Houston's life.

strongly disapproved of Houston's actions. He left Washington in disgrace. He later said that this incident made him realize that he was wasting his life.

Texas and the Fight for Independence

Sam Houston went to Texas, which was then a part of the Mexican province of Coahuila (koh-uh-WEE-luh). Tiana refused to leave Arkansas and go with him. They were later divorced according to the laws of the Cherokee nation.

When Sam Houston arrived in Texas, there were many Anglo settlers there. They were angry at the Mexican government. The settlers wanted more Anglos to come to Texas from the United States.

Six Flags Over Texas

The flags of six nations have flown over Texas. At various times in its history, the state has been under the governments of France, Spain, Mexico, the Confederacy, the Republic of Texas, and the United States of America.

Six flags fly over many sites in Texas.

The best known early Anglo, or white, settler was named Moses Austin. Mexico granted Austin land, and he arrived in 1820. His son, Stephen F. Austin, took charge of the land when Moses died. Today, Stephen is called the "Father of Texas" because he brought many settlers to Texas.

Settlers went to Texas looking for good land at affordable prices.

They wanted to change strict Mexican laws that made it difficult for U.S. citizens to settle in Texas. They also wanted a school system. And they wanted Texas to be a separate Mexican state instead of part of Coahuila. The settlers were not planning a rebellion, but a few Texans were calling for war. General Antonio Lopez de Santa Anna was the dictator of Mexico. A dictator is a ruler who has total control over a country. Santa Anna demanded that the

24

**General Antonio Lopez
de Santa Anna**

Texans who supported war with Mexico be turned over to him. By then, Sam Houston could see that war with Mexico could not be avoided. In November 1835, Houston was appointed major general of the Texas army. He immediately organized the military preparations taking place in Texas.

On March 2, 1836, Texas finally declared itself independent from Mexico. Sam Houston celebrated his forty-third birthday the same day. Meanwhile, Mexican troops had arrived in the small Texas town of Gonzales. A band of Texans successfully drove them out. The Texans then made their headquarters in the Alamo mission buildings in San Antonio. The Texans decided to defend the mission from the approaching Mexicans. But this was against Sam Houston's orders. The vic-

The Battle of the Alamo took place on March 6, 1836.

tory at Gonzales made the Texans believe that they could defeat Santa Anna's army. They were wrong.

Sam Houston knew the Texans couldn't win. He set out with a group of soldiers to rescue them, but he didn't reach the Alamo in time. There were many more Mexicans than Texans. During the final battle with the Mexicans on March 6, every defender of the Alamo (189 men) was killed.

26

The Alamo

The Alamo was established as a Spanish mission in 1718. It didn't become famous, though, until after the March 1836 battle. Today, it is located in the heart of San Antonio. It's open to visitors seven days a week. There is no charge for admission.

The Alamo is really a group of buildings that includes the church, a barrack where soldiers slept, the Alamo Museum, and a library. The Alamo is called the "Shrine of Texas Liberty." (A shrine is a holy place.)

Thousands of people from throughout
the world visit the Alamo each year.

After the Texans' defeats at the Alamo and Goliad, Sam Houston led the army east to escape Santa Anna.

After the fall of the Alamo, Sam Houston ordered General James W. Fannin and his four hundred troops to abandon their fort in nearby Goliad. But Fannin did not obey the order. On March 27, he and his men were killed by the Mexicans.

People angered by the massacres at the Alamo and Goliad joined Houston's army. They wanted

28

revenge against the Mexicans. But Houston led his army east, toward the Gulf Coast of Texas, and away from Mexico. Behind them, the Mexican army moved deeper into Texas. Citizens wanted Houston to fight Santa Anna's army. Instead, Sam Houston kept moving his troops away from the Mexicans. He knew that the only way his small army could win was to find the right place to stand and fight. Meanwhile, The Runaway Scrape slowed down his army's movement.

Sam Houston found the place his troops could defend on the San Jacinto River, near present-day Houston. On April 21, 1836, shouting "Remember the Alamo!" about 750 Texans attacked 1,350 Mexicans. The Mexican troops were at siesta, their afternoon nap. Only two Texans died and twenty-three were wounded, but 630 Mexicans were killed. Santa Anna and 729 other Mexicans were captured. The Texan troops demanded that the Mexican leader be killed, but Houston refused. He wanted to keep Santa Anna as a hostage to make the Mexicans move out of Texas.

One of Sam Houston's greatest achievements
was leading the Texas army to victory against
Santa Anna in the Battle of San Jacinto.

The Runaway Scrape

Texas settlers feared that they would be killed by the invading Mexican army. They loaded their belongings onto wagons, horses, or their own backs, and headed east. They, too, were trying to keep ahead of Santa Anna's army.

It rained a lot in the spring of 1836, and the roads were very muddy. The people clogged the roads and fought for places on ferries that were crossing rivers. They made it difficult for Houston's army to move quickly.

This marker, located on U.S. Highway 90 near Dayton, Texas, commemorates the Runaway Scrape.

STATE HISTORICAL SURVEY COMMITTEE

TEXAS

THE RUNAWAY SCRAPE

FAMOUS FLIGHT OF TEXIANS TO ESCAPE SANTA ANNA'S INVADING MEXICAN ARMY. TALES OF THE ALAMO BUTCHERY ON MARCH 6, 1836, AND THE CONTINUING RETREAT OF GEN. SAM HOUSTON'S ARMY PROMPTED COLONISTS TO ABANDON HOMES AND PROPERTY AND SEEK REFUGE IN EAST TEXAS.

FAMILIES LEFT BEDS UNMADE, BREAKFAST UNEATEN, AND RAN FOR THEIR LIVES, TRAVELING IN WAGONS, CARTS, SLEDS, ON FOOT, OR BY HORSEBACK, DROPPING GEAR AS THEY WENT.

MANY LIBERTY COUNTIANS REMAINED AT HOME UNTIL MID-APRIL, HELPING REFUGEES STRUGGLE TOWARD THE SABINE IN ORDER TO CROSS TO SAFETY IN THE UNITED STATES. TERRIBLE HARDSHIPS PLAGUED THE RUNAWAYS TRYING TO FERRY THE SWOLLEN TRINITY RIVER. IN RAIN-SOAKED CAMPS MANY CHILDREN DIED OF MEASLES AND OTHER ILLS. WADING THROUGH FLOODED BOTTOMLANDS, THE WAYFARERS CAME WITH RELIEF TO THE PRAIRIE AND THE SAMARITANS IN LIBERTY.

AFTER RESTING A FEW DAYS, TENDING THE SICK, AND BURYING THE DEAD, MOST OF THE WANDERERS MOVED ON TOWARD LOUISIANA. EAST OF LIBERTY STRAGGLERS HEARD THE CANNONADING AT THE BATTLE OF SAN JACINTO ON APRIL 21, 1836. FEARING THAT SANTA ANNA'S LEGIONS HAD WHIPPED THE RAGGED TEXIAN FORCES, THEY HURRIED ON, BUT SHORTLY HEARD JOYFUL NEWS: "TURN BACK, TURN BACK". FREEDOM HAD BEEN WON FOR THEM BY SAM HOUSTON'S ARMY.

(1972)

From President to Governor

After the Battle of San Jacinto, Texas was ruled by a temporary government. By September 1836, elections were held to choose a new president and to approve a constitution (a statement of laws for the Republic of Texas). Sam Houston was elected the first president of the republic. He was sworn in on October 22, 1836. He ran the government from a log cabin in the city of Houston.

As president of the republic, Sam Houston wanted the U.S. government to officially recognize Texas as an independent country. He also wanted to find

Houston, Texas

Houston, Texas, was founded by two brothers who named it in honor of General Houston. They planned a large city with churches, a court-house, a market, and a building for Congress to meet. They hoped that Houston would become the capitol of Texas. (In 1839, the capitol of Texas was permanently moved to Austin, a city in central Texas. Austin was named in honor of Stephen F. Austin.)

Today, Houston is one of the two biggest cities in Texas. Many ships dock there, bringing goods from foreign countries. There are also many oil refineries nearby. It is a big, busy modern city.

**Sam Houston takes the oath of office
as the first president of the Republic of Texas.**

ways to pay the heavy debts Texas had taken on during the fight for independence.

During his presidency, Sam Houston did much to improve Texas. He succeeded in getting official recognition of Texas from the United States. With effective use of troops, he made the borders of Texas safe from invasions by Mexicans and attacks by Indians. Houston managed Texas's money carefully. He was able to repay the republic's debts. Under Sam Houston's leadership, Texas flourished.

In 1838, Houston's term as president ended. According to Texas law, he could not be president again right away. Vice President Mirabeau Lamar became president.

Houston did not like the way President Lamar ran Texas. Lamar let Texas get heavily into debt again. Sam Houston was especially bothered by the unfair treatment that Lamar gave the Indians.

Margaret Lea, around the time she married Sam Houston (1840)

In 1839, Lamar allowed Texas troops to attack a peaceful Cherokee camp. The Cherokee were driven north out of Texas, and into the Indian Territory (Oklahoma).

Sam Houston's personal life, however, was more peaceful than his political life. In 1840, he married Margaret Lea. She was a loving wife, and Houston finally found happiness. The couple had eight children.

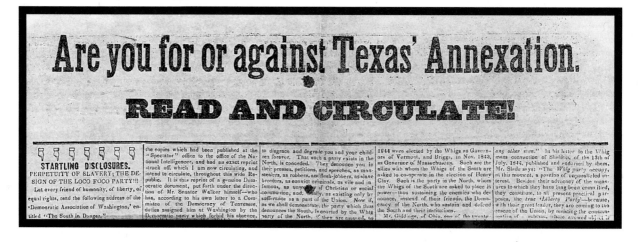

STARTLING DISCLOSURES.
PERPETUITY OF SLAVERY; THE DESIGN OF THE LOCO FOCO PARTY!!!
Let every friend of humanity, of liberty, of equal rights, read the following address of the 'Democratic Association of Washington,' entitled "The South in Danger."

Notices discussing annexation (statehood) were circulated throughout Texas before citizens finally voted for statehood on October 13, 1845.

When President Lamar's term as president ended, Houston again ran for president. He was elected and took office in 1841. During his second presidency, Texas fought off another invasion by Mexico. But Houston knew that Mexico would attack again as long as Texas was a poor, independent nation. Texas would either have to submit to Mexico or turn to another country, such as the United States, for help. Houston worked hard to interest the United States in making Texas a state. He also worked to convince Texans to vote for statehood. On December 29, 1845, Texas officially became the twenty-eighth state in the Union.

36

Sam Houston paused for this photograph in 1852 while serving as a U.S. senator.

Sam Houston completed his second term as president in 1844. In 1845, he was elected as one of Texas's first senators. He traveled to Washington, D.C., and served three terms in the U.S. Senate.

By the 1850s, slavery was becoming a troubling problem in the United States. The country was divided among those who thought slavery should be outlawed, and those who thought it should be expanded into other states and territories.

As anger over the slavery issue increased, slaves throughout the South—including these slaves on a Texas cotton plantation—continued their work.

Like many people in the Southern states, Sam Houston owned slaves. He was not against slavery, but he spoke out against the anger that existed among the states over the issue. Many people in Texas who owned slaves were angry that Houston did not fully support expansion of slavery. When he ran for governor of Texas in 1857, he was defeated. People were so angry at Sam Houston that they forgot that he was the hero of San Jacinto.

Following his defeat, Houston slowly rebuilt his popularity in the state. He traveled throughout Texas explaining his opinions on slavery. He also talked about the importance of being part of the United States. Houston's efforts paid off. In 1859, he was elected governor of Texas.

By 1860, many Southern states were threatening to secede from (to leave) the Union over the slavery issue. They were determined to form their own country where slavery would be allowed. Sam Houston called these threats "secession madness." He saw great danger to Texas if it left the Union. When Texans voted for secession in January 1861,

CHARLESTON

MERCURY

EXTRA:

Passed unanimously at 1.15 o'clock, P. M. December 20th, 1860.

AN ORDINANCE

To dissolve the Union between the State of South Carolina and other States united with her under the compact entitled " The Constitution of the United States of America."

We, the People of the State of South Carolina, in Convention assembled, do declare and ordain, and it is hereby declared and ordained.

That the Ordinance adopted by us in Convention, on the twenty-third day of May, in the year of our Lord one thousand seven hundred and eighty-eight, whereby the Constitution of the United States of America was ratified, and also, all Acts and parts of Acts of the General Assembly of this State, ratifying amendments of the said Constitution, are hereby repealed; and that the union now subsisting between South Carolina and other States, under the name of " The United States of America," is hereby dissolved.

THE

UNION

IS

DISSOLVED!

THE EXTRA IN CHARLESTON WHICH ANNOUNCED
THE ORDINANCE OF SECESSION
(Reduced)

On December 20, 1860, the front page of
the *Charleston* (South Carolina) *Mercury* newspaper
announced "The Union Is Dissolved!"

Secession

On December 20, 1860, South Carolina was the first state to secede from the Union. Mississippi, Florida, Alabama, Georgia, Louisiana, and Texas soon followed. Together they formed the Confederate States of America (the Confederacy). As a result, the Civil War began on April 12, 1861.

Sam told his wife, "Texas is lost!" He knew that Texas would have to join the Southern states in the war against the Northern states. Sam didn't believe that the South could win the Civil War.

When Texas seceded, Sam Houston was ordered to swear loyalty to the Confederacy. He refused. As a result, the Confederacy forced him to give up his position as governor.

On July 26, 1863, while the Civil War was still raging, Sam Houston died of pneumonia at his home in Huntsville, Texas. At the time of his death, his great leadership and achievements for Texas were overshadowed by his insistence on loyalty to the Union.

Sam Houston died in this house (modeled after a steamboat) in Huntsville, Texas, on July 26, 1863.

Sam Houston died without knowing the lasting fame that would be his in Texas and throughout the nation. The Civil War ended in 1865. As peoples' memories of the war faded, they began once again to recognize Sam Houston's achievements. Not only had he freed Texas from Mexico, but, as president of the Republic of Texas, he had established a strong government and a safe country. And he had led Texas to statehood. Today, he is remembered as one of the most remarkable military and political figures of the 1800s.

**The San Jacinto Battle Monument is a 570-foot (174-meter)-
tall reminder of Sam Houston's leadership of Texas.**

In Your Community

Sam Houston played such an important role in the development of Texas that a city is named for him. Is there anything in your city named Houston? Does it have any relation to Sam Houston?

Who was an important person in the history of your community? Is the town or city you live in named after a famous person who once lived there? If you're not sure, visit

Timeline

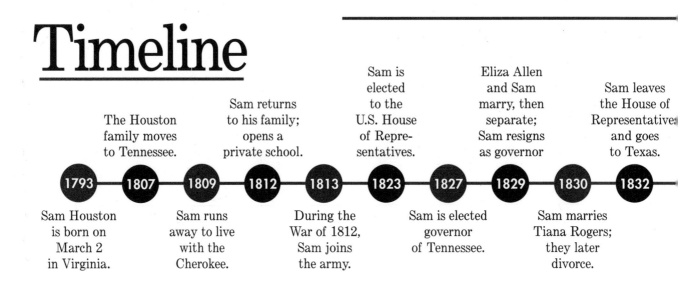

The Houston family moves to Tennessee.

Sam returns to his family; opens a private school.

Sam is elected to the U.S. House of Representatives.

Eliza Allen and Sam marry, then separate; Sam resigns as governor

Sam leaves the House of Representatives and goes to Texas.

1793 — **1807** — **1809** — **1812** — **1813** — **1823** — **1827** — **1829** — **1830** — **1832**

Sam Houston is born on March 2 in Virginia.

Sam runs away to live with the Cherokee.

During the War of 1812, Sam joins the army.

Sam is elected governor of Tennessee.

Sam marries Tiana Rogers; they later divorce.

your local library. The librarian can help you find information about the history of your community.

Once you've learned about the people who settled your community, how can you teach others what you know? Perhaps you can write a report for school. Or write a play about the settlement of your community. Give your friends parts in the play and ask an adult to videotape it for you!

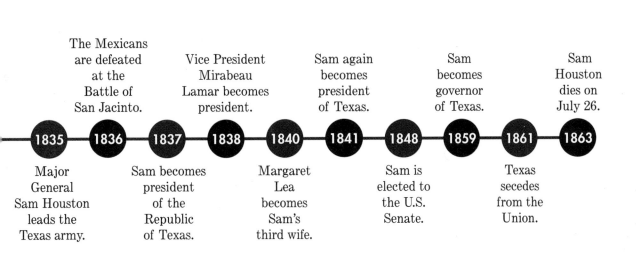

The Mexicans are defeated at the Battle of San Jacinto.

1835 — **1836** — **1837** — **1838** — **1840** — **1841** — **1848** — **1859** — **1861** — **1863**

Vice President Mirabeau Lamar becomes president.

Sam again becomes president of Texas.

Sam becomes governor of Texas.

Sam Houston dies on July 26.

Major General Sam Houston leads the Texas army.

Sam becomes president of the Republic of Texas.

Margaret Lea becomes Sam's third wife.

Sam is elected to the U.S. Senate.

Texas secedes from the Union.

To Find Out More

Here are some additional resources to help you learn more about the life of Sam Houston, the Cherokee, and the state of Texas:

Books

Fradin, Dennis Brindell. *Texas.* Children's Press, 1992.

Fritz, Jean. *Make Way for Sam Houston.* Putnam, 1986.

Lepthien, Emilie U. *The Cherokee.* Children's Press, 1985.

Santella, Andrew. *The Battle of the Alamo.* Children's Press, 1997.

Wade, Mary Dodson. *I Am Houston.* Colophon House, 1993.

Organizations and Online Sites

City of Houston, Texas
http://www.ci.houston.tx.us/history/
Take a virtual tour of the city, view historical photographs, and get links to other sites in the city named for Sam Houston.

Sam Houston
http://www.lsjunction.com/ people/houston.htm
A biography of Sam Houston and links to other sites.

Sam Houston the Man
http://info.lib.ak.edu/cruiser/ silver.html
Includes pages about Sam Houston as a young school-master, Houston and American Indians, Houston and technology, Old San Jacinto, and other topics.

Sam Houston Memorial Museum
19th Street and Avenue N
Huntsville, Texas 77341-2418
http://www.shsu.edu/~smm_www/
Includes a chronology of Sam Houston's life, quotes from Houston, and a virtual tour of the museum grounds and Houston's home.

San Jacinto Battleground State Historical Park
3523 Highway 134
La Porte, Texas 77571-9773
http://www.tpwd.state.tx.us/park/
Take a tour of the battleground, and find out about park activities and nearby attractions. You can see the San Jacinto Monument, and get information about the annual reenactment of the Battle of San Jacinto.

Index

About the Author

Judy Alter lives in Fort Worth, Texas, where she is director of Texas Christian University Press. A novelist and children's author, she is the mother of four grown children and is currently responsible for two large dogs and two cats.

Ms. Alter was born in Chicago, but she has lived in Texas for thirty years. She has absorbed the history of the state and its heroes, such as Sam Houston. Much of what she writes is about Texas, and she wishes that some native-born Texans wouldn't say that you can't be a Texan unless you're born in the state. "I'm a Texan in spirit," she says.

WS JUL 1 9 2000